A Book Of Foolishness for Kids

by

James A. Coffeen

Art by

Niria N. Diaz

Things to think about when you don't have
anything else
you'd rather do

Don't bother reading straight through,
just read

anything that looks interesting.

I didn't write it in one piece,

so why should you

read it that way?

Acknowledgements

My wife Mary Helen Coffeen was in at the start, editing and encouraging me in writing the poems that grew into the book.

I thank Grace Douglas in Brisbane, Australia, who pointed out poems that were good for her then age of seven. Grace now has the title "Kid Editor."

Since then I have added poems that are like the ones she approved.

James Coffeen
Houston, Texas

Table of Contents

A Cat

A cat, you see, is a cat.
It isn't a rat, not a doormat,
Nor a bat, not that!
A catfish, no, but it does love it
To eat, of course, cooked or raw.
Not a catcall but often as loud.
Nor a catcher or cattle.

It's only just a soft little cat.

A Kid Like Me

If you're a kid like me,
You have problems.
Wouldn't it be nice to be grown
And not have those problems?
But the grown-ups act

Like they have problems.
Surely they don't,
Not like mine.
Nah!

Dirt

This dirt underfoot, what is it made of?

Well, it's made of lots of rock ground up
By storms and things, of dust that blew in,
Stuff from old plants, like roots, and twigs,
Old dry leaves, and bodies of bugs.

And it's all ground up and mixed real fine
Mostly by worms, good ol' earthworms.
Till it's just dirt
Like we all know.

It's Just a Game

If you play in the yard and are told to come in
"But it's my turn next, got to see if I win."
"No, come in now, it's just a game.
You can play again later, it'll be the same."
But in the house you must be quiet,
Dad's watching a game and can't miss a play.
You know you can't tell him it's just a game
That he's not even playing, so how can he win?

SHHH'

No, you'd better not say that it's just a game.

Of Course

When do we come back?
Why, after we've gone
— of course.

But when do we go?
After we've come back
— of course.

And that's the whole course
— of course.

Deep Dirt

How deep is the dirt,
how far can you shovel?

You can go down
Till you get to bedrock

And far down below that
There isn't any dirt

Why not, what happened?
When it got deep down underground

The stuff above it
Smushed it and squooshed it
Till it was all rock.

Ickle

If you have a pickle
Just a little lick'll
Make you start to tickle,
Or maybe just be fickle,
Cutting with a sickle.
Just for a nickel.

Mud

If dirt's all those things —
Twigs and leaves and bugs
And their cast-off wings
Bits of rock and slugs

Then what is mud?

Wet dirt, that's all
Just dirt that's wet.

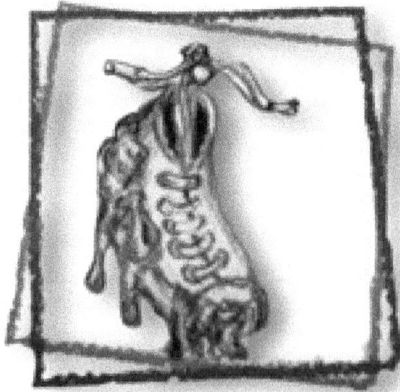

What Do You Know?

I know.
I know what I know.
I know what I know I know

Do you know?
Do you know what I know?
Do you know what I know you know?

Well, I don't know.

When and Where

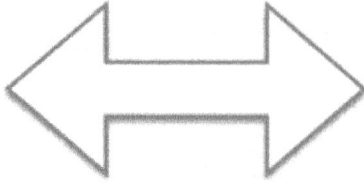

When are we going? Where?

Where are we going? When?

Why Now?

I could have been born
A hundred years ago
Or a thousand,

Or I could be born
in an age yet to come.

But I'm here now
Just right now

Isn't it strange?

This and That

Where is this?
Right here, that's where.
And where is that?
Why it is over there.
Has to be.

How about now and then?
Now is when it's happening.
Then is some farther time.
Maybe it's been. Or yet to come.

That's how it is, with this and that,
And with now and then.

Hot and Cold

How hot is hot? How cold is cold?
The soup is hot. You'll see when you taste it.
The stove is hot. You'll burn your finger.
The steel is hot. It runs like water.
The soup is cold. It's lost its flavor.
The stove is cold. The water won't boil.
The steel has cooled from white to red.
So how hot is hot, and how cold is cold?

It all depends on how hot or cold
You're talking about, or thinking, or reading,
Or writing.

If This Is Near, how Far Is Far?

The ant passed near the beetle,
Didn't bother it a bit.

The ball came near the batter,
He could hear it whistle by.

They had a near collision,
Barely a foot apart.

Houses can't be closer
Than thirty feet between.

We're getting near the city,
Be there in an hour.

Why?

Why, Indeed?
Why not?
Why, why, why?
Why me?
That can't be why.
If not, why not?

If You Dig Straight Down

If you dig straight down, they say,
Clear through the Earth, you'll be in China.
But after half way down,
you're digging up.
You couldn't do it, but if you
could,
Where would you come up?
Look on a globe of the Earth.
From the U.S., you'd come out wet,
In the Indian Ocean, right below you.
From England, the Pacific Ocean.
From Australia, the Atlantic,
Between North America and Africa.
Couldn't anybody do it? Yes, some
People in Argentina and Chile
Would come out in eastern China.
So they can keep the saying.

Let's take an example that's easier
To picture. If you were in Antarctica,
At the South Pole, and you dug
Straight down, would you get to China?
No, to the North Pole, of course. Another sea,
but frozen.

How can all that be?

It's really really
simple —

We've got a lot of
ocean,

A lot more than we
have land.

So most places you
would dig

You'd come out in salt
water.

How Do You...?

Eat with one chopstick,

Cut with one scissor,

Grasp with one plier,

Or chew with one tooth?

Can't do it, can you?

Running

My nose is running,
and I can't catch up.
But I did catch cold.

When I Grow Up

When I grow up, I'll
Go to bed when I want,
Get up when I'm ready,

I'll eat what I want,
When I want to, and
Not be told what
I can and can't do.

When I grow up
I'll be able to do
Whatever I
want.
No one will order
Me around any more.

I wonder why the grownups
Complain so much.

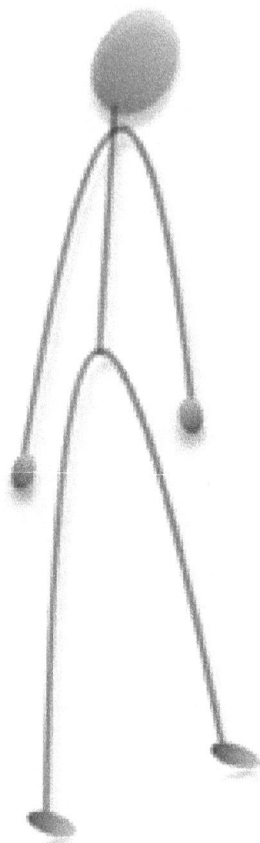

Things that Are Not

An iPad is not as soft
As most other pads.
Don't rest your head on it.
Or sit, or plump it up.

A clothes-horse is not
For you to ride on.
It just will not go
Faster than a four-leg table.

That computer mouse
Doesn't care for cheese.
You can't unlock a door
With those computer keys.

My Dog's Name?

Must be a bark in his tone of voice
To his friends and relatives.

He probably tells me,
But I never understand.

He understands me, though,
When I call his name.
But I don't think he has a name for me.

I was always told that people were the only
Ones that could think,

But I am sure that my
dog thinks.

That Word "We"

A couple of kids
Are walking along.
When they meet
A friend. One says,
"I have just enough money
"So we can go
"To a movie."
Who could go?
The two, or the three?
What was the third one to
think?
What was the third one
to say?
"Goodye, enjoy the
movie."
Or
"Thanks, I'll be glad to go."
Isn't it awful?

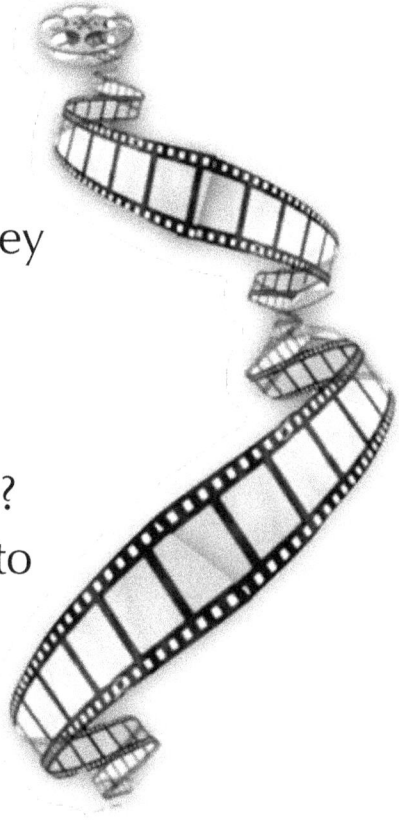

Skills

When you learned to read
A grown-up taught you.
Many things you learned
Grown-ups taught you.

But when the question is
Something about computers,

Who then does the teaching?
Could it sometimes be you?

I can teach you

Alternates

When and where
And this and that,

Now and then, us and them,

Good and bad, here and there,

High and low, which and what,

Toss and turn, accept and spurn,

Start and finish, and diminish,

Land and sea, you and me.

Even These

Sun's nearly down,
It's evening, evenly between
Daylight and dark.

We've evened up,
So I don't owe you, and you
Don't owe me.
I climbed the mountain even to
the top. That's the way it
is, even so.
But not even-tually

A Place Called "Here"

There's a place I know and it's
Called "Here"
A different kind of place, it's
Always with me. If I go to the next room,
Or far out to sea, It's right
Where I am. It goes as far and as
Fast as I go. But it's not just a place,
It's the center of my world.
Other places are interesting but
In a far-off kind of way.
Here is more real, it may be raining
there, but if It's raining here I get wet.
Here has the weather,
There has the news.
Here is where I'm reading, there,
Farther down the page.

How Far Is There?

Suppose you want to know
How far there is, at all.
Imagine the universe,
With our galaxy
And its billions of stars,
And on beyond
To the billions of galaxies.
Does it go on forever,
Or come to an end?
What does it mean
To go on forever?
If there is an end
What is beyond it?
Too much for you to imagine,
Isn't it?
And for everyone else,
Too

Kitty Feelings

People used to think
If you were lying down and your cat got
On your chest
And kind of pumped with its
Front feet, that it was stealing your breath !

How foolish !
What it's probably showing is
That it loves you.

If I Could Fly

What if -- I could fly.
Not with wings, but a
    simple device.

Strap it on and go.
Like swimming underwater.

Land on a tree limb -- uh
        oh
Could break under me, and
    Only flight prevent a fall.

There are some telephone wires.
Couldn't land there, wouldn't hold me.

And maybe, they aren't telephone.
If they have power, and I touched two --
    Bzzzt, and bzzzt, and bzzzzt !

But with care,it could be fun,
Soaring and swooping, and scaring people.
Land on a rooftop -- of a flat-top building
Not on a house, with its sloping roof.

Not as much freedom
As it looked like

At first.

String String

If you string beans
Do they make a longer string?
Longer than a string of string beans?
But when you sit down
and you string
string beans,they don't
have their strings any more.
String a-ling, a-ling a-ling,

A-ling.

Cats and Tigers

A kitty-cat is soft and friendly,
A tiger is big and fierce.
It's nice to hold a kitty in your lap.
Wouldn't want to meet a tiger on
the road.
But if you were a mouse, you might not
fear a tiger. But oh, a cat, so fierce and deadly.
So what is the difference, between the two?
Just size, nothing but how big they are.
If they switched sizes, you'd hold
A cuddly stripy tiger in your lap.
Pet it and hear it purr.

purr purr purr

And go see a big ol' kitty in a zoo.

The Trip and the Rip and the Trip

I was starting on a trip
One that I'd been waiting for.

But then I slipped and did
That very thing -- trip,
Got a bruise and my clothes a rip
And couldn't make the trip.

A slip, a trip, and a rip
Can spoil a trip.
Without that trip and rip, the
trip
Would have been -- just a trip.

As the old saying goes,
"There's many a slip
Twixt the cup and the lip."

A and An, And

There is a difference between
An ape and a nape,
An uncle and a knuckle,
A butterfly and flutter by,
A crouch and a grouch,
A mouth and a mouse,
Mention and tension,
Fourth and forth.

Flammable and inflammable --
No, there isn't.

Friends

Strange about animals.
A dog will chase a cat up a tree.
But at home, your dog and cat
Can be best friends.

All sorts of other animals
That one would have chased
Or eaten the other
Can be good friends.

It happens in the wild too, sometimes,
As you may have seen on YouTube.

What Do You Wear?

What you wear depends.
Nothing at all when you re taking a bath

And for a short time when changing clothes

Wear pajamas at night.
All that's with your family.

Around other people
You stay dressed all the time.

Except for a bathing suit at the beach.
And it feels good,
Doesn't it?

The Great Change

You were a little kid, and someone would
Take you up on a lap, and read to you.

But then the change came.
You started in school.
You learned your phonics and then --
You could read for yourself!
You could pick up a book, or a comic,
Or newspaper, or a cereal box at breakfast,
And read what was there!

That was the great change.
From a kid who was read to,

To being able to do
Your own reading.

Where To?

Where Are We Going?
I don't know, ask the leader.
Going? I'm leading the way
The group wants to go, of course.

But they don't know, they
Are following. How can the leader
Follow from in front?
Well, the rest of us are busy following;
We don't have time to lead.
We are following a leader
Who is going the way
He thinks we want.

What a leader! What followers!

Where will it lead us all?

Have You Read?

The article about the particle?

The mail about the sale?

The book about the crook?

The joke about the smoke?

The tale about the whale?

The announcement

about the pronouncement?

The word about the bird?

The order about the border?

The news about the dews?

The clause about the laws?

The paragraph about the telegraph?

The discourse about the race course?

The elements about the elephants?

That One-Tree Isle

In the cartoons
You often see a tiny isle
With just one tree.
A palm tree of course,
To put it in the tropics.
The isle is just
Big enough for one to a few people.
And small enough
To show the water all around
So we can tell that it's an island.
Just enough isle, just enough tree
To set us up for some joke
About a lone and isolated
Person or more.

In a simple cartoon.

Why School?

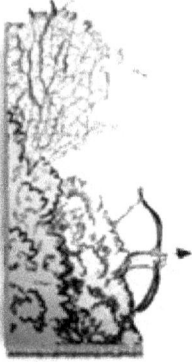

Why do we have to go to school?
For the same reason that
When people were wild animals
The kids had to learn to find food,
And other skills so when they Were
grown they would know
Enough to raise their own kids.

Now a kid needs to learn other
Things for the same reasons.
To earn a living when they are grown
So their kids will have
Enough to eat and clothes
and doctors
And a roof over their
heads.
The things to learn are
different, But the reasons
are the same.

A Rhyme This Time

Epilog and catalog
And rotten log
And big ol' dog

Penmanship and ocean ship
And ownership
And friendship.

House and mouse
And pretty blouse
And soaking douse.

Right hand and hired hand
To beat the band, and

On the other hand.

When I Was a Kid

When I was a kid, I took peanut
    butter sandwiches
    To lunch, and
Learned to read by
    phonics,

Case Cycle Chase

Each letter with its sound,
Or more than one sound,
And you can't tell which,
But have to remember.

Neck

I still like peanut butter,
And phonics.

Thick and Thin

The line
Is getting
Longer, so the
View is getting thicker
And pretty much thicker than
It was, and now about the same
And once again the same as then
But starting to thin a bit, so
It would lose that thickness
And get thinner than that
Thinner yet until it
Is clearly losing
Thickness as it
Proceeds
Until
Thin
And
It
Is
The
End of
The book

www.ingramcontent.com/pod-product-compliance
Lightning Source LLC
Chambersburg PA
CBHW060625030426
42337CB00018B/3197